PACIFIC NORTHWEST

SMITHMARK

For rights information about the photographs in
this book please contact:

The Image Bank
111 Fifth Avenue, New York, NY 10003

Producer: Solomon M. Skolnick
Author: Jennifer Grambs
Design Concept: Lesley Ehlers
Designer: Ann-Louise Lipman
Editor: Joan E. Ratajack
Production: Valerie Zars
Photo Researcher: Edward Douglas
Assistant Photo Researcher: Robert Hale
Editorial Assistant: Carol Raguso

This edition published in 1994 by
SMITHMARK Publishers, Inc.
16 East 32nd Street, New York, NY 10016

ISBN 0-8317-8841-0

Printed and bound in Singapore

SMITHMARK books are available for bulk purchase
for sales promotion and premium use.
For details write or telephone the Manager of Special Sales,
SMITHMARK Publishers, Inc.,
16 East 32nd Street, New York,
NY 10016; (212) 532-6600.

Title page: *A tidepool at Cannon Beach,
Oregon is home to small crabs, jellyfish,
and other marine life swept in by ocean
tides.* Opposite: *Silhouetted seastacks
near Rockaway, Oregon reveal a rugged
coastline.*

W ashington, Oregon, and Canada's British Columbia largely make up the region known as the Pacific Northwest. The best known and most populated area runs along the Pacific coast, west of the Cascade Mountain Range. Known as the "wet side," water rules this region which the Pacific Ocean, lakes, rivers, and year-round drizzle keep damp and brilliantly green.

Overcast skies are a part of life here and people call sunny days "sunbreaks" because of their infrequency. Surprisingly enough, more sunglasses are sold in the Pacific Northwest than anywhere else in the United States. Some joke that this is because people lose their dark glasses between sunbreaks, but in reality the Pacific Northwest is an outdoor recreational paradise with enough skiing, sailing, hiking, and other outdoor activities to warrant sunglasses even on seemingly gray days.

Approaching the Pacific Northwest from the east, there is a surprising change in vegetation and landscape. While much of the Midwest and the states west of Minnesota to western Washington have long stretches of flatlands made up of working farms or tumbleweeds, the region west of the Washington Cascades to Seattle has lush forests and moist air, making visitors feel like they are in another land.

Although the coastline of Cape Kiwanda, Oregon looks treacherous, it is actually one of the few places in the world where boats can be launched into the surf from a sandy beach that extends for miles south of the cape.

Clamming is a favorite pastime along Oregon's sandy shores. Below: Crowds gather to witness the meticulous construction of sandcastles during Cannon Beach's Annual Sand Castle Competition.

The east side or the "dry side" of the Cascades, however, deserves recognition. The dry flatlands are complimented by mountains, rivers, lakes, and acres of ponderosa pine, creating a landscape reminiscent of the Old West. Although there is dust and volcanic ash from the 1980 volcanic eruption of Mt. Saint Helen's, it is warmer here than it is farther west and the dryness contributes to magnificent snow falls in winter.

A delicate iron bridge spans Yaquina Bay at Newport, on the Oregon coast. Sunsets are beautiful here as hues of orange, red, and gold wash over the sky and water. Right: *Fishing fleets ride at anchor in Yaquina Bay at Newport, Oregon.*

As expected, there is a regional rivalry between the east and west side inhabitants of the Cascades. But like competitive but loving siblings, they remain family members of the Pacific Northwest, a region open enough in attitude and landscape to accommodate both.

Deciding on a starting point for travel in the Pacific Northwest region isn't easy, but it's hard to go wrong with Oregon, which has 350 miles of rocky cliffs and sandy beaches that satisfy just about anyone.

Most of Oregon's seaside towns focus on fishing, lumber, and tourism as sources of trade. Fishing boats, oyster beds, and large freighters picking up shipments of lumber for export are common sights along this stretch of the Pacific.

A few towns on the coast have gone in a different direction, however, like Cannon Beach in northern Oregon. Named after a cannon that washed ashore in 1846 when a U.S. Navy schooner became shipwrecked, Cannon Beach is known as an artist's community, where galleries and cafes line the streets off one of the most beautiful beaches on the West Coast.

Preceding page: *Cape Foulweather, near Newport, is one of many points in the northern region of the Pacific that gets blasted by the big storms that roar out of the Gulf of Alaska.* This page, top to bottom: *Yaquina Bay Lighthouse, near Agate Beach, stands over 96 feet tall and is believed by some to be haunted. The coastline near Otter Rock, Oregon offers miles of craggy, wave-eroded formations including Devil's Punch Bowl, where the water appears to boil as incoming tides rush through its openings. Agate Beach at Newport, Oregon is one of the finest spots in the world for hunting these semi-precious stones.*

The crashing waves off of Shore Acres State Park, near Coos Bay, Oregon, attract wave and storm watchers. Left: Coos Bay, Oregon is a large coastal lumber port where deepwater vessels load their holds with northwest lumber.

Yellow, prickly gorse blooms in a field off Bandon Beach. Among the offshore rock formations is Face Rock, thought by many to resemble a human face. Below: Skunk cabbage in bloom near southern Oregon's Cape Blanco, so named for its chalk-white cliffs.

Every year, many of the town's artists join thousands of visitors on this wide and sandy beach for the Sand Castle Competition. A summer arts program sponsored by a nearby college is also held here, with people painting and sketching natural scenes such as Haystack Rock, one of the most dramatic looking seastacks along the coast.

South of Cannon Beach, west of the cheddar cheese-producing town of Tillamook, is the Three Capes Loop which features three jutting promontories: Cape Meares, Cape Lookout, and Cape Kiwanda. Each cape boasts a state park where pounding surf and strong winds have eroded the rock and trees along the water into interesting shapes.

Sea lion and whale watching bring many people to this area. Storm watching, a pastime growing in popularity, also draws crowds as more and more people book cozy hotel rooms in the winter to watch the big storms roar in from the Gulf of Alaska. Gale force winds and crashing waves create a dramatic picture which can be safely enjoyed on land. After these storms, the beach turns into a beachcomber's paradise; all sorts of treasures wash up on shore, from seashells and driftwood to glass Japanese fishing floats.

Cape Foulweather is another dramatic headland that is noted for its rugged scenery. Rising 450 feet above the waves, this cape provides the highest coastal vista in Oregon.

To the south of Cape Foulweather is the picturesque town of Newport. A number of things make this town notable: it is the hub of Dungeness crabbing, shrimp fishing, and oyster farming; it has an attractive waterfront that mixes commercial fishing with art galleries and restaurants; and it has a beach full of agates.

Agate Beach is covered with hard, semiprecious stones of striped or clouded coloring. When the surf washes over these stones, they become dark and shiny and look as though they belong in a treasure chest rather than on a beach.

The Yaquina Bay Lighthouse is also nearby. Built in 1871, it overlooks jagged rocks and mounds of driftwood. The tides and currents are strong in Yaquina Bay, making sailing treacherous and a lighthouse useful.

South of Yaquina Bay near Florence is yet another unusual sight for this generally wet region—41 miles of giant sand

This page, top to bottom: *Clouds float over the Painted Hills at the John Day Fossil Beds National Monument in Oregon, where seashells, teeth, and bones can be found dating back to over 40 million years ago. The John Day River flows past the base of Sheep Rock. Gray, green, and brown tones streak the hills at the John Day Fossil Beds which were covered at one time by an ancient sea. Opposite: Lower Oneonta Falls in the Oneonta Gorge Botanical Area, Oregon.*

Rising over 11,000 feet, Mt. Hood is the highest point in Oregon. Its slopes are a popular playground for skiers and hikers. Below: South Sister is part of the Three Sister Range in the Cascade Mountains. To the left, Mt. Bachelor appears in the distance. Opposite: Colorful wildflowers cover the alpine meadows of Three Fingered Jack in Central Oregon, one of many snow-streaked peaks in this area.

dunes. Known as the Oregon Dunes National Recreational Area, it is a magical place of undulating hills of sand. Footprints quickly disappear as wind smooths over the surface of the sand, so it's advisable for explorers to stop by the visitor's center for maps and information before entering the dunes.

Looking more like the Arabian desert than a Pacific Northwest beach, the dunes stand apart geologically because of their easily erodible sandstone makeup. The ocean, in fact, has pushed the sand farther inland with its tidal action and strong, whipping winds keep the area dry and in constant motion. Most of the coastal mountains, in contrast, consist of basalt, a dense volcanic rock that began to take shape millions of years ago when shifting plates caused volcanos to develop along this edge of the continent.

The port town of Coos Bay can be found south of the dunes. More industrial than Newport, Coos Bay's large harbor is a perfect place for deep water vessels to pick up lumber. Like Newport, fishing is good here, especially for the sport fishing crowd, whose favorite catch is bass.

Preceding pages: *A chain of volcanos viewed from Middle Sister in the Cascades. From left to right are Mt. Washington, Three Fingered Jack, Mt. Saint Helens, Mt. Jefferson, Mt. Hood, and Mt. Adams.* This page, above: *Built during the Depression by local craftspeople, Mt. Hood's Timberline Lodge is a rustic masterpiece of stone, timber, and ironwork.* Left: *When autumn arrives in Oregon's quiet Hood River Valley, the orchards at the foot of Mt. Hood turn crimson and gold, creating a dramatic ring of color around the snow-covered mountain.* Opposite: *Mt. Hood provides a majestic backdrop to the city of Portland. Oregon's largest city, Portland lies at the head of the Willamette Valley, where the Willamette and Columbia Rivers meet.*

Pictures and neon signs recalling early pioneer days are a common sight in Portland. Left: An elaborate "Portland" sign marks the site of the city's Performing Arts Complex, a three-theater complex used for a variety of performances.

Adjacent to Coos Bay is Shore Acres, an outstanding state park. Before Oregon owned Shore Acres, it belonged to a local lumber baron who tended the floral landscape with great care.

South of Coos Bay is cranberry country. The town of Bandon is Oregon's cranberry capital, with 900 acres devoted to growing this tart Thanksgiving treat.

Cape Blanco, near Bandon, is the farthest point west on the Oregon coast. The cliffs of Cape Blanco are a chalky white and the sand is black, unlike the tan-colored sand spanning the rest of the coast.

Oregon is a state filled with natural wonders. Crater Lake National Park in south central Oregon is a giant crater that contains the deepest and perhaps the bluest lake in North America. Surrounded by sheer cliffs, the lake is the result of a volcanic eruption that took place some 6,000 years ago. It is a favorite place to camp for those who prefer a high and dry landscape.

The John Day Fossil Beds National Monument in central Oregon is another natural wonder. The monument consists of three main areas: Sheep Rock, Painted Hills, and Clarno, which together encompass 14,000 acres.

This page, top to bottom: *Portland's annual Rose Festival features a parade, as well as other activities like the Hot Air Balloon Classic. Oregon's Capitol Building in Salem is a stark white structure topped by a golden pioneer. Tom McCall Park, in the heart of Portland, is a place where residents can relax, play, and picnic.*

Clockwise, from left: *The Manor is one of many lovely old buildings on the campus of Portland's Lewis and Clark College. The Park Blocks District of Portland was set aside by early settlers to protect the area from commercial development. Pittock Mansion, a French Renaissance residence, was built in the early 1900's by the founder of Portland's daily newspaper.*

This high desert is actually an ancient seabed. Since the late 1800's, thousands of fossils have been discovered that tell of prehistoric times. Many of these fossils are now part of the Smithsonian Institute in Washington, D.C., as well as other natural history exhibits worldwide. Amateur fossil collecting is no longer allowed in the John Day Fossil Beds, although scientific research still continues.

Bend, Oregon sits just east of the Cascades next to the Deschutes river, about half way between Crater Lake and the rural cattle town of John Day. Although a river rushes through Bend and snow-capped mountains rise in the distance, much of the land is dry and flat.

A number of all-season resorts in the nearby mountains and along the river make this area an active playground for skiers, white-water rafters, and fishermen. Mt. Bachelor, for example, challenges skiers seven months of the year. And when the snow isn't falling, hikers and mountain climbers are traversing its slopes.

Other nearby mountains and parklands also draw crowds. Three Sister Wilderness, which is part of the Oregon Cascades, features

This page, top to bottom: *A statue of Sacajawea, the Indian guide who showed explorers Lewis and Clark the overland route to Oregon, stands tall among the trees in Portland's Washington Park. "Portlandia," the second largest hammered copper statue in the world, kneels in front of the Portland Building. Nestled in the heart of Portland's Washington Park, the Japanese Gardens feature classic oriental retreats with a multitude of flowering bushes and trees.*

Steam rises from the crater of Mt. Saint Helens. In 1980 the mountain blew its top in a volcanic eruption, losing 1,300 feet of its cone. Below: Hot lava and ash covered miles of terrain during the Mt. Saint Helens' eruption, causing parts of the mountain to resemble a barren moonscape.

triplet volcano cones that are
covered with snow for at least ten
months of the year. During August
and September, wildflowers in the
higher elevations come into full
bloom, turning these alpine
meadows into a hiker's paradise.

Portland is Oregon's largest
city with nearly 400,000 inhabitants. Two rivers intersect here:
the mighty Columbia to the north,
which acts as a natural border with
Washington, and the Willamette,
which divides the city, east from
west.

*Mt. Adams, east of Mt. Saint Helens,
pierces the clouds at more than 12,000
feet above sea level.* Right: *Oregon's Mt.
Hood casts a reflection on Lost Lake.
Snow-covered for most of the year, skiing
often continues on its upper slopes well
into July.*

Mt. Rainier, Washington's most celebrated and highest mountain at 14,420 feet, takes up all of Mt. Rainier National Park which fans out for miles.

Leafy, open, and clean, Portland has acres of parkland; Washington Park is the largest park with dense, forested areas and a Japanese garden. Portland also enjoys a dramatic backdrop of mountain peaks: the Coastal Range lies to the west and the Cascades to the east.

Mt. Hood dominates Portland's skyline. In addition to being a landmark, glacier-capped Mt. Hood supplies Portland with its drinking water. It is a popular getaway for outdoor enthusiasts because it offers hiking and skiing year-round. Mt. Hood's Timberline Lodge is one of the most beautiful old lodges in the world.

Oregon's capital city is Salem, located in the heart of the Willamette Valley. The city is surrounded by fertile farmland, giving it a gentle, pastoral look. With Oregon's rich history of explorers and pioneering spirit, it seems only fitting that its Capitol Building should be topped with a golden pioneer.

Murals and statues depict famous explorers such as Captains Meriweather Lewis and William Clark who were sent by Thomas Jefferson in 1804 to explore the shores of the Pacific. Maps, descriptions of wildlife, and scientific information came out of that journey, as well as a deep respect for Native Americans whom Lewis and Clark befriended with the help of an Indian guide named Sacajawea.

This page, top to bottom: *The Cascade Mountains are relatively young and rugged, offering the serious hiker good trails which lace through just about every nook and cranny of the range. Icy, blue lakes, like Image Lake at Tenpeak Mountain, are a refreshing sight to hikers in the high country of Glacier Peak Wilderness area. Smooth with ice and snow, the Laconte Glacier is one of many spectacular glaciers in the Washington Cascades' Glacier Peak Wilderness area.*

Mt. Baker's snowy peaks pick up the color of the setting sun. Near the Canadian border in the North Cascades, this mountain was given the name "Great White Watcher" by Native Americans in this region. Below: One of the smaller bodies of water in the North Cascades National Park region, Hidden Lake is surrounded by rocky mountain peaks that contrast with the mother-of-pearl sheen of the lake.

Rocky beaches and secluded coves make up much of Washington's San Juan Islands. 42 islands are undeveloped and open to campers who can reach them by boat. Below: Snow is a rare sight in the rainy environs of the San Juan Islands. Here, the Kiln Lighthouse blends in with the surrounding white landscape.

Directly to the north of Oregon is Washington. Seattle is its largest city with about 500,000 people and is situated approximately halfway between Vancouver, British Columbia and Portland, Oregon. Because of its location, Seattle is an ideal stopover for travelers heading north or south.

Seattle, like Vancouver and Portland, has a deep water port where freighters load and unload containers of cars, grain, and other

Rich agricultural land in western Washington's Skagit Valley provides many of the tulips and daffodils sold on the open market. During the spring, thousands of acres come alive with red, white, and yellow blossoms. Right: *Clusters of logs are grouped together in Everett's Port, north of Seattle, for eventual transport and processing.*

Clockwise, from left: *The Space Needle was built in 1962 for the Seattle World's Fair. Chief Seattle, a local Indian hero, raises an arm in friendship Seattle's Washington Mutual Tower rises above its downtown neighbors.*

goods. Tacoma, Seattle's closest neighbor to the south, also has a thriving port. Working harbors of these cities are highly competitive, vying for Pacific Rim business with Japan, China, and Australia. International trade with the Pacific Northwest offers the close proximity of seaports and airports to Asia, as well as relatively new harbors which are capable of adjusting to new technologies and growth.

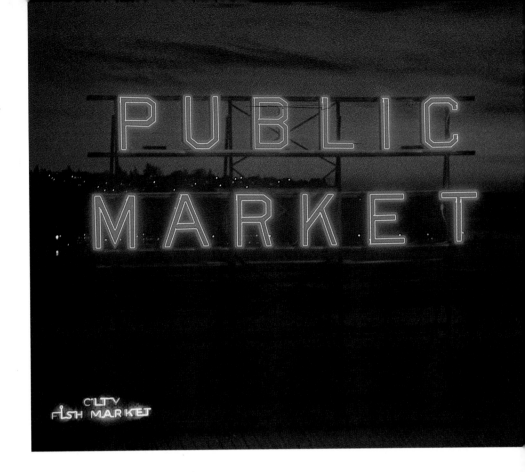

Seattle's Pike Place Market is located in the heart of downtown, near the city's waterfront. Below: The steamship Virginia V *docks at Pier 55 on Seattle's waterfront. This grand old vessel is a popular party boat for sunset cruises around Puget Sound.*

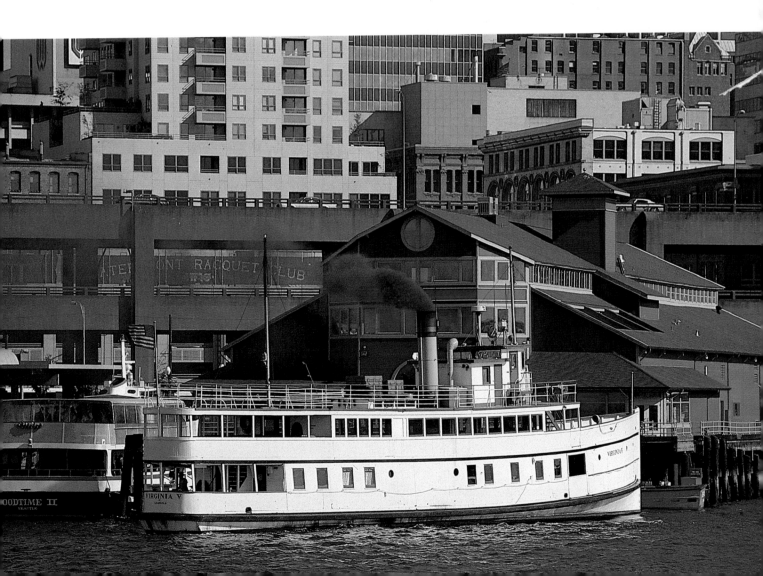

Clockwise, from left: *Once the tallest skyscraper west of the Mississippi, Seattle's Smith Tower now stands under the shadow of other buildings twice its height. The Washington Mutual Tower is one of Seattle's newest and most popular skyscrapers, its imaginative design and iridescent blue exterior making it a welcome addition to the city's skyline. South of Smith Tower is Pioneer Square, with shops, restaurants, galleries, and cafes.*

Pioneer Square, for example, is Seattle's oldest settlement. Now an historical district, the area is full of turn-of-the-century buildings that hark back to Alaska gold rush days.

Gold was discovered in Alaska in the late 1800's and Seattle served as a stopover for many prospectors heading north to find their fortunes. The town profited from their return, when they would spend their money on merchandise and entertainment. As a result, Seattle grew larger than Portland, building to serve a rich and restless clientele.

The World's Fair in 1962 was another turning point for Seattle. Billed as the "Century 21 Exposition," the fair focused on a vision of the twenty-first century. The Space Needle, a Seattle landmark, was built with this vision in mind. Resembling a space ship aloft, this 605-foot structure is now an integral part of the city's skyline, along with the towering presence of the Cascades and the Olympic Mountains.

While Seattle is the urban hub of the Puget Sound area, there is a web of islands and peninsulas that gives this part of the country much of its charm. The Olympic Peninsula, for instance, is covered with an exotic rain forest that contains some of the last old growth trees in the world. These towering forests are covered with wispy moss and vines that feed off the rich soil and damp environment. 12 to 15 feet of rain descend

The oldest Presbyterian church in Washington is located in the Victorian seaport town of Port Townsend on the Olympic Peninsula. Right: *Victorian Square in downtown Port Townsend is one of many red, brick buildings on the waterfront that give this town its character.*

The Blue Glacier on Mt. Olympus in the Olympic Mountains seems to reach a dramatic end, but changing temperatures keep its mounds of snow and ice in motion. Below: The Hoh Rain Forest on the Olympic Peninsula features old growth trees and an abundance of lush greenery, from giant ferns to berry bushes. Moss grows on many of the tree trunks.

One of the most dramatic areas on the Washington Coast is Rialto Beach on the Olympic Peninsula. Below: A giant seastack rises up from Rialto Beach during low tide.

each year on the Olympic Mountains that run down the middle of the peninsula. Without a doubt, this is one of the wettest places in the world.

Port Townsend on the northeast corner of the peninsula is one of the most attractive towns in this area, as well as a hopping seaport. The town is known for its arts community and climate. It sits in a "rain shadow," protected by the Olympic Mountains. As a result, it misses much of the precipitation that affects the region, receiving only 20 inches of rain a year compared to Seattle's 35 inches.

The Parliament Buildings in Victoria, British Columbia take on a magical glow at night when they are illuminated by miniature lights. Left: The elegant Empress Hotel next to Victoria's inner harbor is a popular spot for high tea.

The San Juan Islands to the north of Seattle are another geographical gift to the Pacific Northwest. Washington state ferries sail through narrow saltwater channels as they navigate this 172-island archipelago scattered over 179 square miles at the eastern approach to the Strait of Juan de Fuca. Filled with evergreen trees and coves, the San Juan Islands are very quiet—only about ten are populated.

Just west of the island of San Juan is Vancouver Island where Victoria, the capital of British Columbia, is located. Ferries between Seattle and Victoria run daily, making it an easy trip for those who want to experience both the American, Canadian, and British influences of this region.

Some say Victoria is more English than England, which in some respects appears to be true. British double-decker buses and tudor architecture can be seen, and high tea is served in the lobby of the Empress Hotel, Victoria's most regal residence. But what clearly sets Victoria apart from the British Isles is its Canadian Indian heritage, apparent throughout its streets and parks. Indians were here well before the British arrived; totem poles and landmarks bearing tribal names still mark the land.

This page, top to bottom: *Vancouver, British Columbia has the second largest Chinatown in North America. An elaborate entrance beckons tourists to the city's best Asian restaurants and markets. A paradise for horticulturalists, Buchart Gardens near Victoria, British Columbia has 35 acres of some of the most beautiful flowers in the world. Victoria Fable Cottage Estates in Victoria is a fantasy world of fairy tale houses and animated scenes.*

Northeast of Victoria on the mainland is Vancouver, British Columbia's largest city. Well over a million people live in this cosmopolitan center, many of whom are from countries all over the world. It's more international than its southern neighbors and as a result has a vibrancy that only a rich cultural mix can provide.

French, Greek, and Hindi are just a few of the languages spoken on the streets and Vancouver has the second largest Chinatown on the West Coast. Oriental delicacies can be found in the numerous open-air markets and East Asian restaurants.

A totem pole depicting a Canadian Indian family or clan towers over Victoria, British Columbia, a city which combines English and Canadian Indian traditions. Below: A brightly painted Kwakiuti bear pole harks back to Canadian Indian tribal roots.

Often referred to as Canada's "gem of the pacific," Vancouver, British Columbia is surrounded by soaring mountains and sandy beaches.
Below: *Situated on a peninsula between Burrard Inlet and the Fraser River, Vancouver is connected by a series of bridges. The Lions Gate Bridge connects Stanley Park and West Vancouver.*

The top of Vancouver's Canada Place Pavilion takes on an ethereal look in the early morning light. Left: The Vancouver Expo 86 "golf ball" has been converted into a center for hands-on science exhibitions.

Vancouver is visually breath-taking. It is surrounded by mountains that look almost close enough to touch. In addition, the city has sandy beaches right in the heart of town, where sunbathers and swimmers can take in the mountain view.

Whistler, about an hour's drive from Vancouver, is one of the finest ski areas in the Pacific Northwest. The town of Whistler sits in a valley between two mountains, Whistler and Blackcomb. Both mountains offer a variety of ski slopes, as well as hiking trails and crystal-clear lakes. Whistler got its name, people say, for two reasons: because of the whistling sound that the wind makes as it blows down through Fitzsimmons Pass between Whistler and Blackcomb Mountains, and because of the high-pitched whistle made by the hoary marmots that make this area their home.

The province of British Columbia is vast, with a spectacular array of mountains, glaciers, plains, coasts, and islands. It is larger than any U.S. state, other than Alaska, and boasts six national parks and 336 provincial parks within its boundaries.

This page, top to bottom: *One of Vancouver's most imposing structures is its City Hall, which has a stone-faced clock. Resembling a walking crab, a modern sculpture stands over a fountain in front of Vancouver's MacMillan Planetarium. Built to house the national government's exhibit at Expo 86, Canada Place is now the city's trade and convention center, as well as a hotel and a cruise ship terminal.* Following pages, left: *Blazing neon signs advertise the many restaurants in Vancouver's Chinatown.* Right: *Gas lamps and red, brick buildings line the streets of turn-of-the-century Gastown, in Vancouver.*

This page: *A statue of "Gassy Jack" Deighton, a saloon proprietor from the early days, stands in Gastown's Maple Tree Square.* Below: *Gastown's historic steam clock lets out a hoot and a rush of steam as it tells the time.* Opposite page, clockwise, from left: *Snow-capped Atwell Peak in Garibaldi Provincial Park is one of many natural wonders in this large preserve, located north of Vancouver. Blackcomb and Whistler Mountains have the longest vertical drops in North America, providing challenging skiing for those with the stamina to take them on. Chairlifts haul skiers from the village of Whistler to the tops of Whistler Mountain and Blackcomb Mountain.*

In the Coastal Mountain Range, Garibaldi Provincial Park has alpine lakes, jagged volcanic peaks, huge glaciers and beautiful snow-capped Mt. Garibaldi, which towers over the park.

The Queen Charlotte Islands off the northwest coast of British Columbia offer beautiful terrain for exploring. Made up of nearly 150 craggy and densely forested islands, wildlife abounds there, from bald eagles to gray whales that pause to feed in Hecate Strait during their migration from Mexico to Alaska. Mist and fog often cover the Queen Charlotte Islands, but their unspoiled beauty draws naturalists from far and wide.

The people of the Pacific Northwest are perhaps best known for their respect and love of their environment. Balancing commerce with conservation has always been a difficult task, but preserving the unspoiled vastness of this region remains a priority. The environment is a key issue and remains on the front pages of area newspapers as a reminder to all that man has the ability to destroy as well as protect the natural beauty that makes this part of the continent a very special place.

Preceding page: *Many of the mountain peaks in Kootenay National Park remain covered with snow throughout the summer.* This page, above: *Crystal clear Lake Magog in Mt. Assiniboine Provincial Park, is surrounded by rugged peaks, including the pyramid-shaped Mt. Assiniboine.* Opposite: *Mt. Assiniboine in the Canadian Rockies.*

British Columbia's Queen Charlotte Islands, north of Vancouver Island, rival Norway's fiords in their natural beauty. **Below:** *The rocky shores of Canada's Queen Charlotte Islands are a favorite gathering place for sea lions.* **Opposite:** *Western cedars are reflected in one of British Columbia's many freshwater lakes.*